my tiny veg plot
Lia Leendertz

Photography by Mark Diacono

PAVILION

First published in the United Kingdom in 2015 by
Pavilion
1 Gower Street
London
WC1E 6HD

ISBN 978-1-91049-605-3

A CIP catalogue record for this book is available from the British Library.

10 9 8 7 6 5 4 3 2 1

Reproduction by Mission Productions Ltd, Hong Kong
Printed and bound by 1010 Printing International Ltd, China

This book can be ordered direct from the publisher at
www.pavilionbooks.com

contents

introduction

Think you don't have enough space to grow your own fruit and vegetables? Think again. This book concerns the tiniest of productive gardens: those that have been squeezed in the most unlikely fashion onto flights of steps, balconies, boats and roof terraces. There is even one in an old swimming pool. Most would have deemed these spaces too tiny to bother with, but they come with a set of determined and often ingenious gardeners that have transformed them into something special. These gardens prove that small is not only beautiful, but it can be surprisingly productive as well.

Gardeners often spend their lives yearning for more space in which to grow a greater volume of crops, but tiny gardens need not be the poor relation of the big patch, or just a stepping stone towards your acre. Small gardens have a huge amount going for them in themselves: they are easy to care for and to fit around a busy life, whereas large gardens and allotments can quickly become overwhelming and all encompassing; and they are near at hand, so that problems with pests and diseases are spotted early and dealt with quickly, and produce is picked when it is at its peak. You will never let a French bean grow past its sweet and compact best, or let a slug strip the whole plant to the ground, when it is positioned in the side return just outside your back door. It is also the case that many of the strongest-flavoured crops are small – think herbs, chillies, garlic – and so it is very easy to create a tiny garden that punches well above its weight in flavours.

Left: The most delicious of edible crops can be fitted into the tiniest of spaces.

Right: Food crops can be beautiful as well as delicious.

And you are not limited to only growing herbs. A great range of vegetables will grow well in containers if given the right care, as will beautiful dwarf fruit trees and bushes, and all will love the extra attention they receive at the hands of a gardener who isn't overwhelmed by a huge garden and all of its attendant chores. In short you can grow a great range of the best quality, most delicious produce from a tiny plot, and all with minimum stress.

This is all possible if you choose crops carefully to suit your situation, and design your garden well with the limitations of your space in mind, and this book contains an array of tiny gardens from which to seek inspiration in setting about such a task. The first chapter is about high-rise growing: those gardens that are wedged into balconies or that teeter on rooftops. These gardens offer both challenging and hugely rewarding conditions: winds and weather can dry out plants and wreak havoc but these gardeners have high light levels and wonderful views to more than compensate their struggles, and all of them seem very happy with their lot. Chapter two concerns urban growing, and all of its gardens have been shoehorned around the architecture of the city: pots arrayed up steps, a roofed veranda for city privacy, and a planter that doubles as a bicycle rack. In chapter three we see the ways in which the smallest of gardens can be used for the greater good, to create community cohesion, to experiment with environmentally friendly ways of growing, and to concentrate fertility in lands with poor soils. Chapter four is about mobile gardens, those in the back of trucks and campervans, all of which exploit to the full the ability of plants to grow wherever they can get sustenance and light. Chapter five is about the tiniest of all gardens, and is for those people who believe they have nowhere they can grow: they are mistaken. There is always some way of growing food and this chapter will show you how. In chapter six we learn some lessons from businesses who grow tiny crops for their amazing strong flavours, and finally in chapter seven we look at some of the tiny gardens that have grown up in some of the most unlikely places: near to or floating on water, on boats and tiny banks. Together these chapters cover a vast array of gardens and gardeners all with one thing in common: they are working creatively with what little space they have, making amazing edible gardens on the small scale.

Left: A clever planter that doubles as a bicycle lock.

This is not just an inspirational book. In addition to the garden profiles, this book contains panels that will teach you the techniques you need to make use of every inch of your space, from planting up edible hanging baskets, to growing herbs in cracks in paving, to supporting and training your crops so that they grow upwards, and thus take up little space on the ground. These panels also discuss the slightly more serious business of watering and feeding – plants in containers are entirely dependent on us for their moisture and sustenance, and unlike their counterparts in the open ground are unable to reach out into the soil for new sources of either during periods of drought, or when one area of soil is depleted of nutrients. Paying attention to watering and feeding is crucial in creating a tiny container garden that grows and crops well and looks thriving and beautiful, and you will find ideas on how to ensure you do this effectively in these practical panels.

But the message this book most wishes to pass on is: don't give up too easily. If you wish to grow your own crops but have convinced yourself that you don't have any space in which to do so, spend some time among these pages. They may make you look at your own space with fresh eyes. There is a certain magic to growing in unlikely places that those with the luxury of space may entirely miss out on. Maybe you can have a tiny salad garden, maybe you can even make a miniature orchard. I hope that you will enjoy looking at these brilliant little gardens, and that you will be inspired by seeing what other gardeners have achieved to create your own tiny veg patch.

Lia Leendertz

Left: Herbs are among the best plants to grow if you have little space: compact and full of flavour.

Right: Even the most unusual crops, such as South American tuber oca, can be grown in pots.

raise 'em high

High-rise spots such as rooftops and balconies can make for the most pleasing miniature vegetable gardens: unexpected oases of greenery and colour. There are few things more uplifting than spotting a thriving garden up among the chimney tops, all unlikely. Greenery up so high carries the mark of a dedicated gardener – without one little could grow for more than a few days so far from nourishing earth – and we all love to see a well-loved space. Lifted out of the shade of neighbouring buildings and trees, these can be some of the lightest and brightest of city gardens, and increased light levels make them surprisingly productive, as plants feed greedily on the sunlight and then convert it into delicious crops.

art and veg meet on a bristol balcony

Nell Nile's beautiful balcony perched high on a Bristol hillside is not the only place she grows food. 'I've got an allotment where I grow flowers and vegetables, but it's a good ten minutes' walk away. That's fine for most vegetables, but this is where I grow the things that really need to be harvested just before you eat them.'

Nell is an artist, and colour and flowers are very important to her. 'I combine all the veg and herbs on the balcony with flowers. It's a bit of an obsession. I like the challenge – finding an oriental leaf that tones in with a calendula, or growing a bright dahlia alongside a bluey-green kale.' This year she has gone big on lettuces. 'I've planted dark, frilly 'Lollo Rossa' lettuce in my hanging baskets in among the pink and coral geraniums. The darkness of the 'Lollo Rossa' sets off the bright flowers, and the lettuces frill out and fill up the gaps, and make it all look full and lovely. I've been so pleased. Lettuces make surprisingly good hanging-basket plants.'

Lettuces also feature in Nell's window boxes, which she has attached to the front of the balcony. They nestle in among surfinias and lobelias. 'I grow mild-tasting green lettuces here. They're the ones I'm most likely to eat in my sandwich. I particularly like the mild, sweet taste of 'Little Gem'.'

In her pots she grows purple basil. 'I love basil and can't get enough of it, and I also love the dark purple foliage of this one. It looks beautiful nestled in among my colourful zinnias.'

Right: There is no shortage of light on Nell's second-floor balcony, high on a hill overlooking Bristol.

Opposite: The colours of Nell's flowers match her beautiful Chinese-silk mural.

Above: Nell sows trays of mixed salad leaves, then eats the thinning.

Above right: Purple basil 'Opal' combined with Nell's favourite flowers, zinnias and geraniums.

style and gardening notes

The balcony is dominated by the huge mural that Nell painted on the back wall. 'It just seemed like such a great blank canvas and a waste to leave it bare,' says Nell. 'I really wanted to do something special with it. I collect old Chinese fabrics and the pattern came from a piece I found. The colours were much stronger when it was first painted, but they've faded with the sun over the years. One of these days I'll paint a whole new design.'

The combination of high light levels and wind makes Nell's pots and hanging baskets hard to keep moist. 'I have to water a lot. The hanging baskets and window boxes are the worst because they're really out in the wind. When I plant, I mix water-retaining granules into the compost and then water every day.'

Nell also grows trays of cut-and-come-again salad leaves up here. 'They wouldn't survive at the allotment with all the slugs, so I grow them here.' She sows a different salad leaf in each shallow tray and harvests them every time they are just tall enough to eat. And of course, she also harvests the basil regularly. 'The basil thrives in the conditions up here and it grows really well. It loves the light. I do have to keep pinching the plants back to a growing point, though, or they quickly go to flower. Pinching them out also encourages them to grow into nice bushy plants, plus you get a regular supply of basil leaves.'

Left: The hanging baskets are filled with geraniums in pink and coral shades, and dark purple lettuce 'Lollo Rosso'.

Above: Nell has create a beautiful spot in which to relax and enjoy the views.

Above: Joel's roof-top allotment.

Opposite left: The allotment shed sits on top of his self-built art and music studios.

Opposite right: Joel loves to cook up on the shed-roof top, with all of his produce to hand.

man on shed

When artist and composer Joel Bird first started creating his extraordinary allotment-roofed shed, he was not entirely convinced it was going to work. 'I was making it up as I went along. I knew I wanted a workspace in the garden, but I've always wanted an allotment, too. I just thought I'd give it a go.' So first, he built his studio and then started working out how to grow food on the roof. 'It's hard to get hold of an allotment in London. There are long waiting lists, so building my own up here, on top of my studio, seemed like the obvious move.'

Joel also has some previous experience of looking after a regular, ground-level allotment, and had found – as many people do – that they are often extremely hard work to look after well. 'It was big and full of couch grass and weeds, and the rules were too strict. It felt like a hard way to go about growing. I thought this might be simpler, and it is.'

Joel comes from Liverpool and his original plan was to use his new space to grow the ingredients for scouse, the famous thrifty and greatly loved Liverpudlian meat and veg stew. 'But I quickly realised that turnips and swedes were so cheap to buy that I might as well grow tomatoes and herbs,' he says. He often cooks and eats up here with his family, enjoying his vantage point across neighbouring allotments from his very own, hand-built plot.

Left: Chillies thrive in the high light levels on the shed roof.

Above: A patch of rhubarb grows direct into the imported soil.

style and gardening notes

The shed itself is constructed in a sturdy but eclectic style, all odd angles and interesting pieces of wood, and a pleasing mixture of new and recycled. As a result, the rooftop allotment has a determinedly irregular shape, too. To make the roof watertight, Joel laid torch on felt. He then needed something to hold on to moisture, so he put down a layer of fabric. 'Just some cheap, ordinary cotton fabric. Like I say, I really was making it up.' Then he added a layer of gravel and finally a layer of soil. 'When I started building, I dug out and saved the soil from the footprint of the shed, so I just replaced it up on top.'

He even laid a turf path on the roof and built raised beds on either side. The depth of soil is around 30cm (1ft) in places, which is enough to help prevent the garden from drying out too rapidly. Joel does need to water during dry spells, but says 'I've been amazed at how well it all works overall.' The shed garden has been such a success that he has since started taking on commissions and building them for other people.

The crops that grow best on the roof are tomatoes and strawberries; they obviously relish the good light levels. Mediterranean herbs are also very happy as they do not mind occasionally drying out. 'But generally I just grow what I like to eat. Everything does really well up here,' says Joel. 'And it's just a special place to spend your time.'

Above left: Potatoes produce well in sacks of compost.

Above centre: Mediterranean herbs don't mind getting dried out occasionally.

Above right: The strawberry patch is one of the best crops.

high among the chimney pots

Below left: It's easier than you'd think to squeeze in a greenhouse to a rooftop plot.

Bottom right: Wendy spends 'hours and hours' relaxing in her garden.

Among the rooftops and chimneypots of Fitzrovia, far above Central London, perches Wendy Shillam's vegetable garden. Despite measuring just 5m x 6m (17ft x 19ft), Wendy has shoehorned in a greenhouse, compost heap, garden office and several beds, all of which jostle around a large skylight. 'I spend hours and hours up here, but not all of it's gardening. I eat my breakfast and pick off a dead leaf or two, or take a break from work and pull a few weeds. People say "It must take so much time!" but I don't come up here to garden. I just come up here.'

Wendy is an architect and knew that the roof was structurally sound enough to bear the weight of the plants. 'Every book you read about roof gardens says you must get an engineer in, but in fact a dead load – which is what plants are – isn't usually a problem. If I wanted a party of 30 people up here on pogo sticks, that would be a different matter.'

She and her husband Mike laid wooden decking tiles and built raised beds in between, then Wendy started planting. 'I had no idea it was unusual to mix flowers and veg,' she says, but she has now spent the last 17 years perfecting pretty and productive mixes that make the most of her tiny space. She has purple beans 'Cosse Violette' with dark purple sweet peas winding through; runner beans with morning glory; and kale 'Red Russian' dotted with purple violas. 'My aim is to grow veg beautifully, but it's not that hard. I think vegetables have their own intrinsic beauty.'

Left: The greenhouse grows tomatoes right into winter.

Below left: Violas mingle among kales, lettuces and chard.

Left: The raised beds are shallow, but support a great amount of healthy growth.

Above: An automatic watering system – topped up with occasional cans – is the secret of Wendy's success.

Right: Wendy uses pergolas and trellis to create height and structure and to make use of every inch of space.

style and gardening notes

Wendy's house was once a dress factory: 'There are six floors and every room has three fireplaces. Three tailors would work around each,' she says. 'That's why there are so many chimneypots up here.' They dominate the roof garden ('I like the way they glow red in the sunset,' says Wendy) and form high walls to the north and south. Despite this, the garden gets plenty of light and Wendy finds she can grow plants here that she could not grow in a previous, darker, ground-level London garden.

She also does well with frost-tender plants such as tomatoes. 'It's very rare to get a frost up here, so the tomatoes in the greenhouse just keep on going. I came out last Christmas morning and picked some.' When she pinches out their side shoots in summer, she pots them on as cuttings and brings them on as new, late plants, to give her a supply of winter tomatoes.

The five large raised beds each have a soil depth of just 15cm (6in), which makes watering crucial. Wendy has set up a drip system: hosepipes run around the garden with drip attachments that allow water to seep slowly out.

She also has a cunning way of keeping her tomatoes well watered. 'I cut the base off the pots and put them in a tray of pebbles. Then I water into the tray. The water-seeking roots spread out into that.' The feeding roots lie at the surface of the compost, so although she waters from below, she feeds from above. It is one of many ways in which Wendy has made the most of her precarious garden location. 'You get such a sense of achievement growing food up here. And I eat the most fantastic crops. You really value them.'

Right: Two of the 1m by 3m (3ft by 10ft) beds on Anne's apartment roof.

hong kong comes down to earth

There aren't a great many places to grow food in Hong Kong. Land tends to be used for skyscrapers rather than vegetable gardens, but when Anne Roberts moved to an apartment in Kowloon, she was delighted to find that it came with its own rooftop plots. 'There's no great culture of growing food in Hong Kong, for obvious reasons,' she says. 'I've always been a keen gardener but it wasn't something I imagined I'd be able to keep up in Hong Kong.'

Below: Anne's tiny allotment is an oasis in built-up Hong Kong.

But the management committee of her apartments has built tiny 1m x 3m (3ft x 10ft) plots into the roof of the building's podium, and has got some farmers to teach the residents to garden. 'It's an educational initiative. Every Saturday a group of farmers visits from the New Territories, to the north of Hong Kong. It's an area full of smallholdings and it's where most of Hong Kong's fresh produce originates. The farmers bring manure and plants, and then help the residents of the apartments with their plots.'

Anne was one of the few experienced gardeners there and had slightly different reasons for wanting to garden. 'I wanted to grow salads. The Chinese are wonderful at all sorts of vegetables but they don't grow lettuce or rocket. I was craving these. I was desperate for some crunchy lettuce in a sandwich. I could buy lettuces from ex-pat shops, but they were flown in from abroad and were very expensive. My little plots have allowed me to grow them for myself.'

Left: Several of the plot holders grow papaya trees.

style and gardening notes

Anne took on three of the tiny plots. The soil is shallow but very workable. 'Every time they come, the farmers give us each a bucketful of manure. It means the soil stays in great condition.' The climate is fairly challenging though. 'In winter it's just a bit damp and grey, like a dull spring day in England. But in summer, it's very hot and humid – often 100 per cent humidity. And then there's the occasional typhoon. You can arrive at your plot and find it strewn with rubbish.'

Most of the gardeners grow Chinese staples such as aubergine, daikon radish, bitter gourds, Chinese spinach and pak choi under the tutelage of the New Territories farmers. All of these plants thrive in these conditions. Anne grows these too, 'but I can buy them anywhere. It's the European-style salad leaves that I most want to grow. Everyone thinks I'm very odd.'

But Anne's plants can prove tricky. 'In summer it's hard to get the lettuces to germinate. They like to be cool and the temperatures here are just too high for them.' Summer heat also leads to many of the green leafy crops bolting. 'It happens so quickly in the hot weather. It seems like a rocket plant can be fine in the morning and have run to flower by the afternoon. I can just about grow spinach if I keep it well watered. I buy my seed from UK seed companies and I choose what to buy just by looking for the words "slow to bolt" in the description.'

Top left and right: Okra and aubergines grow well in Hong Kong's hot and humid summers.

Above: All watering is done by the plot holders, by hand.

get practical: reach for the sky

Look to the vertical to fit more crops into your small space; going skywards takes up very little room. There are lots of crops that climb, so if you have a trellis or railings, it makes sense to use them for support. Even if you don't, you can create your own simple climbing structures very cheaply, to make the most of all that vertical space.

Climbing annual crops include French beans, runner beans and borlotti beans, peas, cucumbers, gherkins and melons. Winter squash and pumpkins can be trained to grow up supports, too. Vines and kiwis are other choices. They are long-lived and will need big pots and sturdy, permanent supports. They will also need their compost topped up each year.

1. Cucumbers are a good choice for growing up railings as they don't grow too large. Plant seedlings in compost in a pot near the railings.

2. Tie them in as the plant grows. Tie a double knot firmly around a railing and another knot loosely around the stem of the plant.

3. Create your own support for climbing beans by filling a large pot with compost and pushing three tall canes into it. Tie the canes together firmly near the top to form a wigwam.

4. Plant a bean at the base of each cane and tie them in as they grow. Again, tie a knot firmly around the cane with another knot tied loosely around the bean stem.

get practical: make a hanging alpine strawberry basket

Plants already filling every tiny corner of your garden? Then start dangling them in hanging baskets from brackets and pergolas. What is more, there are several edibles that do brilliantly when grown this way. Tiny tomatoes such as 'Tumbling Tom' and 'Cherry Falls' will spill over the edges of the basket nicely, dwarf peas will happily grow down rather than up, and all the Mediterranean herbs will cope well with the inevitable occasional drying out. Strawberries and – as here – alpine strawberries are particularly good; the fruits can dangle down prettily, yet are out of reach of the slugs.

1. Balance a hanging basket on a large pot and line it with a hanging-basket liner or with moss.

2. Place a piece of folded plastic sheeting in the base – I cut up a plastic shopping bag. This creates a little well where damp compost can sit to help to prevent the basket from drying out too quickly.

3. Fill with compost mixed with water-retaining granules, but do not over-fill. The granules will swell when wet and release their water slowly.

4. Plant small strawberry runners around the edge of the basket. Three plants for a 30cm (12in) hanging basket is a good rule of thumb, with 10–12cm (4–5in) between each plant. Firm the plants in well and keep the basket well watered as they mature, flower and fruit. Feed regularly with a high-potash feed such as tomato feed or with comfrey fertiliser (see p.102).

urban solutions

You may live in a concrete jungle, but you can still grow food. Look to odd corners to see where you can fit in a few pots: a set of front steps, a back porch, or just a corner of a little garden. City gardens are often shaded by buildings, so it is a good idea to look to those edibles that thrive in shade. And they are generally small and overlooked, so make the most of this by cramming in plants and colour, and giving them all something to look at.

budget back yard

Penny Golightly's pretty little London back yard is bursting with growth, berries and vegetables. It's very much the sort of garden that you would expect has had time, energy and money lavished on it. But in fact, Penny – a freelance writer on finance and thrift – has set herself the challenge of spending just £50 per year on her garden. 'It works out at just under a pound a week,' she says, 'which seemed manageable as this is such a small patch. I set myself the challenge partly because I didn't have any money and partly because I wanted to see what could be done and show others how to do it'. She writes a blog, 'Golightly Gardens', where she describes the many ways she finds to get around her rather extreme budget.

Despite the tight budget, the garden does not seem to be lacking much. Rhubarb, raspberries, cucumbers and tomatoes all rub along together happily in their 3.9m x 9m (13ft x 30ft) space. She bought the rhubarb on eBay for 99p and grew the cucumbers and tomatoes from seed traded with other gardeners, or given away in promotions. 'You can get an amazing amount of seed for free,' she says. 'You just can't be too choosy about the varieties.' The raspberries, on the other hand, were quite the investment – bought on special offer from a local shop, at six canes for £6.95. 'But we've had a bowlful every day for weeks, so they've been worth it.'

'If money was no object,' says Penny, 'I'd love an asparagus bed and more fruit. I'd like to buy some blueberry bushes, but I'll only get them if I can scale back on something else or swap them with someone for some seedlings. My readers would know if I'd cheated.'

Left Penny has packed fruit, vegetables and herbs into her little London garden.

Right: Her lovely garden has been created on a strict budget of £50 per year.

Above: A set of found steps helps Penny to display her plants.

Above centre: Penny makes space for a pot of clover to help to encourage and feed the bees.

Above right: Raspberries are one of her favourite crops, and a long-term investment.

style and gardening notes

Being small and backing onto Penny's terraced house, this garden does have a shade problem. The far end can be in full sun while the half nearest the house is densely shaded. Penny has planted shade-tolerant rhubarb, radishes, oriental leaves and lettuce in the beds close to the house and has saved the sunniest spot for winter squash, tomatoes, cucumbers and other sun-lovers. She has also built a kind of table from found pallets, where she grows chillies, strawberries and herbs. 'Just lifting them up to about hip-height means that they catch more of the light before the sun slips behind the house.'

Above: The crate 'table' brings herbs and chillies up to an easily workable height, and allows them a little extra light.

Right: The mini-greenhouse is the hub of the garden, packed with seedlings in spring.

With space so short, and to make the most of that sunny patch, Penny found a piece of trellis and fixed it to the end wall, so creating a huge new growing area for climbers. She has painted it a shade of duck-egg blue, in common with a number of other features in the garden. 'I often bring found objects in – a set of wooden steps, some pots, the trellis – and I decided to paint them all this colour. It makes the space calmer and I like the repetition. It brings the whole garden together.'

The powerhouse of the garden is the tiny plastic greenhouse near the house, which in spring is packed with seedlings. 'I grow everything from seed or cuttings and never buy in vegetable plants. And I also always sow way too much. It's amazing what you can get hold of if you've got something to swap.'

Left: Penny has used recycled materials throughout the garden.

Above right: Lavender cuttings for a new hedge.

Right: At the shady end of the garden, Penny grows lettuces and oriental greens.

herb heaven on sun-splashed steps

Ellen Hughes so struggled to grow herbs in the shady back yard of her Bristol townhouse, that she instead created a colourful, herbal garden arrayed down its sunny front steps. 'The yard backs onto a grove of trees and has its own sylvan beauty, but the front steps is where the light and colour is,' she says. 'I use the mint and the chives the most, to go with potatoes or other roasted vegetables and I use the herbs in salads.' A window box on the wall is filled with baby lettuce and rocket leaves. 'I work from home so I pick a few leaves each day to go with my lunch.'

The steps are a lovely halfway point between the privacy of the house and the public road. 'We spend much time sitting out on them. It is a great place to people watch. Our street has a large population of students and we watch them arrive, unpack, wave goodbye to their parents, have parties, struggle with the recycling, fall in love, and then pack up again and go home to their parents at the end of the year. Longer-term neighbours join us on the steps for a drink or to have a chat, or to borrow a handful of herbs. Our teenagers sunbathe, my husband drinks coffee and our younger children use them a repository for stones and pebbles collected on walks and holidays. I love it most in the evenings, sitting out watching the sun set and looking to see how much things have grown since yesterday.'

Above: Herbs grow beautifully in full sun.

Above right: Ellen keeps cut-and-come-again lettuce in a window box fixed to the wall.

Opposite left: Wellington boots make the perfect container for growing tomatoes.

Opposite right: Alpine strawberries flourish on the steps.

style and gardening notes

Ellen grows lots of geraniums for colour. 'It is so important to me to have big splashes of colour here, as it is the only place I can grow flowers. Geraniums are easy and they look glorious all summer'. But it is the herbs that she is most delighted with. 'They love full sun and I grow rosemary, mint, thyme, lemon balm, sage, fennel, chives and parsley, all of which I use regularly for cooking and in salads. I grow them for their smell as much as for the kitchen. Each time I go up or down the steps I find myself picking a leaf, rubbing it in my fingers and smelling it or having a taste. On summer evenings scent from the mint and the lemon balm is so fresh.' 'There are also pots of beetroot, alpine strawberries, a trough of salad leaves and a couple of welly boots the kids have planted with tomatoes.

The only downside is watering, which in such a suntrap needs to be done daily in summer. 'We can only fit little pots onto the steps otherwise we would never get bikes or prams up and down them, and little pots dry out quickly,' she says. But generally she finds the size of the garden makes it very manageable. 'It is never overwhelming to look after, we have a busy family household without a huge amount of time for gardening, but our little sunny garden on the steps is manageable and fun and very rewarding.'

Right: The veranda roof supports climbing plants, such as a verdant vine.

Below: Little pots of lettuce leaves can be harvested and taken straight to the kitchen beyond.

lia's rain shelter

This is my own veranda. We moved into our solid 1920s terraced house ten years ago. Houses like this are square, wide and simple, without the fussy angles and corners created by the side returns that some Victorian houses have, so there was our house's straight, sunny back wall, just crying out for a veranda. The idea always was to create a small covered area for sitting out of the rain (I strongly believe that rain shelters should be built into all British gardens).

A happy side effect is that plants really thrive here, and I've found I can grow edibles that I wouldn't be able to grow in the main garden. In a little space like this – the veranda measures 3m x 6m (10ft x 20ft) – everything's noticed and nothing's overlooked, so everything gets pampered. And by growing in pots, everything can have the conditions that most suit it: herbs can grow in well-drained, gritty compost and be watered only occasionally, while fruit trees are in a rich, water-retentive compost and are given bucketsful of water daily when in full growth with swelling fruit.

There is a bigger garden beyond, but to be honest it's often a little neglected. Being compact, the veranda is much easier to keep in lovely condition. And there's another benefit to it being little and under cover: no matter how fiercely the rain's falling I can always pop out for a handful of herbs for dinner.

Right: Lia has packed edible plants onto her veranda, including nectarines, strawberries and scented leaf geraniums.

style and gardening notes

The hardy banana plants in the main garden provide a sub-tropical background, and this has encouraged me to plant big-leafed plants on the veranda, with splashes of colour in between from verbenas and geraniums. Leaves are important here. I grow lots of scented-leaf geraniums, which I use to infuse cakes and custards with delicate floral or citrus flavours. And the veranda has slowly filled up with tender and luxurious edibles that need a little bit of extra care or protection. I grow turmeric and ginger leaves from tubers, and use them as wraps or to make into teas. Being tropical plants they can't take a frost, so they spend the winter in the little greenhouse on the veranda that nestles up next to the house. That's their double layer of protection.

The roof – clear sheets of polycarbonate – also allows me to grow plants that wouldn't grow well in the wider garden, in particular nectarines and peaches. Although these are perfectly hardy, both suffer terribly from peach-leaf curl, a fungus that arrives on winter and early spring rains. Out in the garden, these plants would be completely laid low by this disease, but here they get not a hint of it and thrive. Tomatoes dodge the blight that arrives on the rain in mid- to late summer, too. I also use the uprights of the veranda to grow climbers. I've grown a huge, productive grape vine and a pot full of mashua tubers, which produce climbing stems of nasturtium-like leaves, orange flowers in late summer, and tasty tubers in late autumn.

Left: Peaches love the extra protection.

Above: Unusual crops such as mashua – a South American root crop – thrive here.

Right: Lia grows turmeric and harvests the leaves for wrapping and steaming foods.

Above right: A small greenhouse keeps her supplied with new salad seedlings.

Below right: Tomatoes don't suffer from blight under the cover of the roof.

behind the bike shed

The Plant Lock planters in King Henry's Walk Community Garden are in good company. This is a garden full of innovative planters packed full of edibles. There are rows of variously coloured salad leaves in one huge metallic planter, kale and courgettes in another. Elsewhere potatoes and chillies, edible flowers and carrots all spill from variously shaped and sized containers. But the dual-purpose Plant Lock planters are particularly innovative. They are wide and deep enough to contain enough soil to support a good range of vegetable plants, but they also act as somewhere for visitors to lock their bikes. Strong bars are built into each side of the planters so that two bikes can be chained to each.

The beauty of the design is that it is just the weight of soil and water that holds them in place. Each planter weighs at least 75kg (165lb) when planted up; they are pretty much immoveable, so the people at the community garden did not have to bother with any drilling and fixing into the ground below.

It is a neat solution to two urban problems – the need for more space for greenery and the need to secure bicycles – all in one tiny space. The many people who visit this community garden by bike no longer have to chain their bikes to railings or drainpipes. Their green mode of transport is accommodated in the greenest and prettiest possible way.

Left: Herbs, flowers and vegetables are combined in the Plant Lock planter.

Right: It is sited alongside other large planters full of vegetables.

style and gardening notes

There are two Plant Lock planters at King Henry's Walk, and they are planted quite differently. One is filled with a lush planting of flowers and vegetables. It contains colourful lobelias and nasturtiums, a couple of small cherry tomato plants and a single plant of white-veined chard. The nasturtium flowers and leaves can be picked and eaten in salad, the tomatoes will start to turn red and sweet and ready for picking towards the end of the summer, and the chard leaves can be harvested all summer long, or can be used for winter salad leaves later in the year when other pickings are leaner. It is a good planting for a space such as this, where, along with the other planters, it will be tended to, harvested and watered on a regular basis.

The second planter is a little different however. It contains predominantly thyme and oregano. Both are Mediterranean herbs that thrive in hot, dry conditions and can tolerate drought. In fact, their leaves will become even more pungent and the oils more concentrated when the plants are allowed to dry out occasionally. These plants would therefore make a good choice of planting for any planter in a public place that was less likely to see regular watering. Passersby plucking occasionally at the leaves, plus the odd drenching shower – the sides of the planters are nicely angled outwards, and so can catch a little more rain than a straight-sided planter would – might well be all the maintenance it would need.

Left: Strong bars are built into each side of the planter for locking up bikes.

Left: Another Plant Lock planter is filled with herbs suited to dry conditions.

Below: One bike can be attached to each side of the planter.

a burst of sun in portland

When Gillian Carson moved to her good-sized garden in Portland, Oregon, she wanted to apply the lessons she had learnt from her tiny garden in the UK. 'My first garden was so small that the vegetable plot was the entire garden, so I couldn't afford to have it look less than lovely most of the year. So I had started to experiment with growing vegetables in patterns.' She encountered some naysayers: 'Some people said it just wouldn't work, but it did and it looked fabulous. When I arrived in Portland, I wanted to do the same and to see if it would work as well in this climate.'

She chose one small patch to create this highly intensive and extremely ornamental vegetable garden; her new 'Sunburst Garden' is 5m x 3m (16ft x 10ft) – about a quarter of her entire plot. Gillian has loved the process of 'painting' the pattern with plants. 'I'm a creative person. I like to write and draw and make things, and I think: why shouldn't that overflow into the vegetable garden?'

She now has a long list of design ideas for the future which she plans to try out around the garden, including a circular salad garden, a diamond herb garden, a zigzag cutting garden and a vertical pumpkin and squash garden. 'I suppose I just like to make a garden that's pretty to look at. I've been vegetable gardening for over ten years and I've just got bored with planting in rows.'

Right: Gillian in her Portland garden.

Far right: The sunburst plot in full swing.

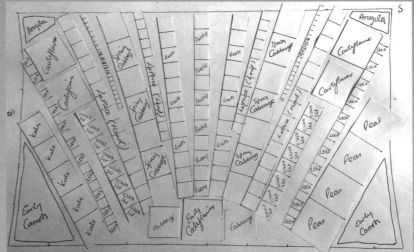

style and gardening notes

'I started by choosing plants like kale, cabbage, cauliflower and onions because I knew that they'd stay in the ground a long time,' says Gillian. 'These were really to give the design some structure. Then I added things like peas and carrots because we eat a lot of them. And lastly, the lettuces, because they're harvested so quickly that you can keep the design looking fresh by planting new lettuces as you harvest them.'

Gillian used her greenhouse to keep a constant supply of lettuce seedlings waiting in the wings, to pop into place as soon as a space arose. 'I also sowed some sweet alyssum to create the archway that holds the sunburst together. This was key to keeping the pattern looking strong all summer long.'

She has a few tweaks in mind for the next time she tries this design, and believes it is important to think about the eventual size of the plants, and to take that into consideration. 'I'm going to put the kale in the centre of the design next time. The plants got quite big very quickly and made the whole pattern look lopsided. If they were in the centre, they'd hold it together.'

But generally she feels that the plan worked well. 'A lot of people ask me, can you really plant vegetables that closely together? The answer is yes. In my experience it's less about space and more about light. Don't have a large plant overshadow a small one. Look at where your sunlight comes from and plant accordingly. You'll get a great crop of vegetables and on top of that, they'll look beautiful as they grow.'

Opposite, above right: Gillian's original plan.

Opposite, top left: First she weeded and prepared the area.

Opposite, middle left: The basic shape was marked out using a board.

Opposite, below left: And then the seedlings were planted out.

Left: The newly planted sunburst garden.

Left: Gillian chose to use long-standing plants that would maintain the sunburst shape all season long.

get practical: crack on with planting

It is always worth seeking out unlikely places to sneak in some extra planting. The cracks between paving may seem insignificant, but choose the right plants, and you can create a carpet of herbs across your path. To achieve this, only old, cracked, badly made paths will do: paths that are perfectly pointed leave no spaces where plants can get a foothold. This is where poorly constructed landscaping comes into its own. I made my path purposely with gaps between each brick, so that I could plant up the spaces.

1. Sprinkle a mixture of topsoil and compost over the gaps in the path.

2. Brush it over so that it fills all the gaps, then firm it down.

3. I used a variegated creeping thyme for this sunny spot but chamomile is another good choice, particularly the creeping, non-flowering 'Treneague'. On a shadier path I would use Corsican mint, *Mentha requienii*.

4. A small potful will give you plenty of pieces, and since these plants root as they run across the ground, it should be fairly easy to pull away pieces with both leaves and roots.

5. Use a pencil or piece of bamboo to make a hole, then plant your rooted pieces into it. Firm the soil around, then water. Water if the weather is dry until the plants have got going.

get practical: give your mint a new lease of life

Mint is perfect for pots, partly because it is a bit of a menace outside of them. When planted out and allowed to range freely, its thick, white roots make a strong bid for territorial gains. They advance, seemingly daily, on borders, smothering out other plants as they go. When they are in a pot, they cannot do that, but it does not stop them from trying. After a year or so in a pot, the roots will have wound their way around the perimeter. This leaves all the energy at the edges. The centre of the plant starts to die back and growth is spindly and weak. But there is a simple trick to revitalise your old, tired plants.

1. Cut off all the long, spindly top growth from your mint.

2. Turn the plant out of the pot. You will see the thick roots around the edge, near the surface.

3. Using a bread knife, slice the plant in two. Be bold: it is almost impossible to kill it.

4. Turn each half around and manhandle it back into the pot the other way around, so that the thick white roots are now in the middle. Use fresh compost to fill any gaps, then firm the surface.

for the common good

Sometimes a tiny garden can be far more than the sum of its parts. Small patches can be used to teach a whole generation of children about food and diet, to introduce a community to growing in an unlikely spot, or to try out alternative growing methods on a domestic scale. Small gardens can also have a big impact where they are used to concentrate fertility and grow highly nutritious crops in areas of poor soils. Never underestimate the power of a small garden, it can achieve big things.

teatime digging for tiny hands

'We talk a lot about poo,' says Sara Limback, with obvious glee. 'With any other group of gardeners I'd call it soil improvement, but this lot find it hysterically funny that they're allowed to play with poo once a month.'

Sara is the leader of Tiny Trowels, a gardening group for pre-school children in Windmill Hill in Bristol. The group is based at the city farm, a sort of urban community smallholding filled with pigs, sheep, goats and chickens. With all those animals, there is never a shortage of soil-improvement material. 'We all wheel our barrows off to the manure pile, load up and bring them back to add to the beds.' With such dedicated and enthusiastic attention, the soil of the Tiny Trowels beds would be the envy of most adult gardeners.

The children's plot is a section of a larger allotment and measures around 3m x 4m (10ft x 13ft). That's just enough space to squeeze in the 20 mums and little ones who might turn up for a session, but small enough to be manageable. It is filled with a series of small, raised beds with paths in between. 'Low raised beds are brilliant for children. They can reach the plants and worms so easily. Raised beds particularly suit the really little ones. From about six months old they can pull themselves up and stand and play with the soil,' Sara says. Many of the mums are nervous about dirt when the children first start gardening: 'The beds stop the babies from completely rolling in the mud but help to get them – and their mums – used to a bit of dirt.'

Left: Ernest and his mum Jen, and Poppy and her mum Katie, enjoy eating raspberries in the garden.

Right: The beds are small enough that the children can lean right across them to dig.

style and gardening notes

Above: Rhubarb growing in a tyre.

Above centre: The children water in their newly planted seedlings

Above right: Flowers such as nasturtiums are important too.

Opposite left: There are always salad leaves growing on the plot.

Opposite right: Jen and Ernest plant out the small plants that Sara has started at home.

The club is not all about random digging. Its purpose is to give children and their parents an opportunity to garden and find out about food. 'Lots of the mums will say, "Oh, she won't eat that", but then we find that the kids will, if they've grown it and picked it themselves.' Ernest, aged four (he's the one in the hat), has tried rhubarb from the plot, to his mother Jen's amazement, and Poppy, also four, has eaten courgettes and courgette flowers, and even chews on the leaves of chocolate mint. 'She said it tastes like After Eights,' says her mum Katie. 'She won't actually eat an After Eight, but she'll eat the chocolate mint.'

The children sow lots of seeds, then plant them out and harvest them. 'Of course it's not quite that simple,' says Sara, 'but a huge amount of work goes on behind the scenes to make it seem simple.' Sara goes home and sows more seed after each session so there are always young plants ready to go. 'The children need to have a sense of achievement.'

There is also a structure to each session, albeit a very accommodating and realistic one. It involves about 20 minutes of concentrated sowing or manuring, 10 minutes of digging for worms and woodlice, 10 minutes of running around and 20 minutes for tea and squash, cake and biscuits. 'Then everyone takes something home to eat – raspberries, strawberries, salad leaves, carrots, beetroots. That's the most important thing. Well, that and the cake.' Who could disagree with that?

politics meets polyculture

Anni Kelsey's unusual bed of perennial edibles has its roots in Anni's politics and in her concerns about food security. 'I always wanted to grow my own food and when I was a teenager, I first became aware of how unsustainable our food chain is.' She found the traditional route of sowing annual vegetables in spring just too hard going. 'I had an allotment, and I grew annuals, but it was too much work, especially with a young family, so I started looking for another way.' Anni found it in perennial vegetables – plants that will grow again year after year, rather than having to be sown and nurtured as baby plants through spring, which can be one of the most unpredictable times of year.

'When I discovered perennial vegetables, I started getting hold of every plant I could find and looking for advice. There are plenty of people growing them but most seem to be doing it on a large scale. I'd love to have a decent-sized smallholding some time, but I don't have it now, and neither do many people, so I had to adapt. I wanted to show that ordinary people with an ordinary amount of space can also grow these crops.'

The siting of Anni's bed also limited its size. It was created out of an expanse of communal lawn that is shared with other neighbours 'I can't bear lawn and I really hate mowing. I'd fill it all with plants if I could, but we decided this was a size that wouldn't bother the neighbours too much.'

Far left: Anni's perennial border.

Left: Fennel and carrots have been left to flower in the border opposite the bed.

style and gardening notes

To create the bed, Anni dug up the turf and turned it over, then added compost, clippings and whatever organic material she could find to build up the level of the soil, before planting into it. She regularly adds all her dead plant material and lawn clippings. They rot down where they fall. 'I refuse to waste anything with fertility potential,' Anni says, 'which is what you're doing if you remove your grass clippings. Everything has to be fed back into the soil.' But she does hide the clippings with an edging of woven hazel, which is another neighbour-pleasing measure. With the garden sited on the side of the Long Mountain in Powys, building the bed up has helped to improve the terrible soil. 'The soil is clay and full of shale. I didn't want to try digging it, so I had no choice but to build it up.'

The planting is a polyculture – lots of different plants mixed together – which helps keep plants healthy as it confuses the pests. Anni has perennial kales and Welsh onions, artichokes, burdock root, skirret ('a root vegetable with a taste something between a carrot and a parsnip'), daikon radish, mashua (an unusual tuber crop from the Andes) and alpine strawberries. In among these are a few annual vegetables – courgettes and broad beans – and some flowers – pot marigolds, cosmos and dahlias. 'But the dahlias are edible. You can make the tubers into a rösti.'

The bed is extremely low-maintenance, 'I watered the artichokes once and I've weeded out some buttercups, but apart from that, it's just a matter of tipping the clippings on. They have to go somewhere anyway! The whole ethos of this bed is literally about doing nothing, but getting as much as possible from it.'

Below: Anni has also created an even smaller perennial planting in a pot at the foot of her steps.

Below centre: Oca, lettuce and dill grow together well.

Below right: Mashua in the perennial border.

Opposite left: Anni mixes some edibles such as broad beans in with the perennials.

Opposite centre: Rat's tail radish produces roots and edible seed pods.

Opposite right: Courgette, growing among the perennials.

Right: Potted apple trees were donated to the garden.

Below: The apple trees are underplanted with herbs to make the most of the space.

Rub these leaves and sniff them. Thyme is used in cooking to give food a good taste. It is said that if you eat a lot of it you can see fairies, and Shakespeare said the fairies come where the wild thyme grows." This thyme is not wild, but canned in Brentford. Sorry.

fully booked with fruit and veg

Outside Chiswick Library, in a space once usually occupied only by a taxi or by an opportunistic shopper's car, now lies a beautiful, small but productive edible garden, just 2m x 3m (6^1/$_2$ft x 10ft). 'It looked bleak,' says Stella Hawkins, library manager for three libraries in the borough of Hounslow, 'Just a stretch of concrete and the bike racks. We were keen to commandeer the area.' The librarians were helped by Abundance London, an organisation initially set up to collect unwanted fruit from local fruit trees and make use of it. 'The people at the Chiswick House Kitchen Garden had some spare trees and offered them to us,' says Sarah Cruz, co-founder of Abundance. 'So we offered them to the library and helped them create this garden.'

The library leapt at the chance to use this new outdoor space in all sorts of ways. 'We made a straw-bale maze to tie in with the children's summer reading theme, "Mystical Maze". It's not quite Hampton Court, but the kids love it. We've run activities there and had storytelling sessions and a performance poet. The children make little paper fruits, butterflies and other drawings, and hang them from the trees.' The vegetable garden has its own signs that encourage passersby to harvest and nibble, and Stella believes this is helping to attract people to use the library. 'The library used to be seen as a middle-class enclave. We've got a brief to draw in hard-to-reach members of the community, and families with difficulties. The garden's helping us to do that.'

Right: The vegetable patch was once used by taxis.

style and gardening notes

Other than a small border running alongside the library where the group have planted artichokes and berries, the rest of the garden is built over tarmac. This impenetrable base posed problems that required nifty solutions. The library's low front wall by the pavement serves as one edge of the main vegetable bed, with pieces of wood hammered together to make the other three edges. This was filled with compost that will need to be topped up each year, and was then planted with beans, tomatoes and nasturtiums. There is no watering system, but Stella says this isn't a problem: 'Some of the librarians have really taken to caring for the garden. Some parts have been fairly aggressively watered, but everyone's learning.'

The donated trees live in large blue hessian-wrapped tubs and Sarah has underplanted them with herbs – lemon verbena, chives, sage and thyme – to make the most of the limited space. The one job that no one has to concern themselves with is harvesting. The signs that encourage library users and passersby to pick and try the crops appear to have been very successful; eager hands pluck at the beans and tomatoes as soon as they show any sign of ripeness.

'Part of the library's remit is about encouraging public health, and here we're demonstrating just how easily you can grow some of your own fresh food, and that you can do it in a small space – even in just a tub. A lot of our users are under-fives. They've got no idea of the connection between growing and eating. The library garden demonstrates that link beautifully.'

Left: The garden is alongside the street and passersby are encouraged to pick produce.

Above: Straw bales encourage children to play.

Below left: The garden fulfils part of the library's educational remit.

Below right: Visitors to the library enjoy harvesting the crops.

through the keyhole in lesotho

Lesotho isn't the easiest place to grow vegetables. The terrain is high and rocky, and the climate is extreme: very hot in summer and very cold in winter, with heavy downpours and hailstorms. The country – entirely surrounded by South Africa – imports the vast majority of its food.

Mankutloang Monmaheng has always grown her own maize, but with the help of British charity Send a Cow, she has developed a 'keyhole garden', which allows her to grow a range of far more nutritious crops. Keyhole gardens are basically circular raised beds. They are particularly useful for farmers in areas with infertile soil as they provide a small, concentrated area of rich soil. Locally available materials are always used to build up the structure: for instance, farmers can use plastic bottles filled with sand instead of bricks or stone, which makes the technique hugely accessible. 'Now I can grow spinach, leafy vegetables, carrots, chillies, tomatoes, beans and peppers. The keyhole garden has helped me increase my range of crops. Now, whenever I feel like eating, I eat,' says Mankutloang.

The keyhole garden is so called because of two features – a slot in the side, which acts like a little access path into the middle, and a 'compost basket', a deep hole at the centre. Mankutloang drops all her kitchen waste into the compost basket, waters it during dry spells and covers it with dry sticks to prevent evaporation. As this waste matter rots down, it keeps the rest of the bed moist and rich in nutrients, easily maintaining this little island of fertility.

Opposite: Mankutloang with her keyhole garden.

Below: The soil in Lesotho is poor and many crops do not grow well in it.

Above: Beetroot growing in the keyhole garden.

Above right: Keyhole garden building is a community activity.

style and gardening notes

Keyhole gardens are among several techniques that Send a Cow encourages Lesothan farmers to try in order to increase productivity. The larger aim is to increase families' ability to earn a living and so bring back men and boys from mining jobs in South Africa. Although keyhole gardens are particularly useful in harsh climates such as this, they are a great way to grow food in less extreme conditions, too, and they are particularly useful where space is tight. They take a bit of setting up (in Lesotho this is done by support groups of local farmers), but once in place, they are beautifully low-maintenance and highly productive.

To make her 3m (10ft) wide bed, Mankutloang and her support group started off by marking out the area. They took two short sticks joined by a length of string, pushed one stick into the soil and used the other to draw a circle with a 0.5m (20in) radius on the ground. They did the same to draw a second circle with a radius of 1.5m (3ft). Posts were pushed into the ground around the inner circle and secured with string to form the compost basket. They then started to build up the outside wall with stones, building in a V-shaped path. The inner basket was filled with compost and the bed with a mixture of compost and topsoil, sloping down from the basket to the walls. The slopes were planted up with vegetables, and kitchen scraps and water were poured into the centre. Mankutloang is a convert: 'You'd be crazy not to grow vegetables. You can eat what you've produced yourself. It's the best thing you can do, and this is the best way.'

Above left: Mankutloang is delighted with her crops.

Above right: Chard and peppers grow well.

get practical: the hows and whys of underplanting

Underplanting is a great way of fitting extra plants into a small space. It works particularly well around large, long-term plantings in pots, such as dwarf fruit trees, where there is an expanse of compost simply crying out for planting. Herbs, like the mint I am using here, not only make terrific underplantings but also work as companion plants: the volatile oils in their stems and leaves help to deter pests, while their flowers draw in pollinators. Dwarf rosemary, for instance, is a good choice for underplanting a dwarf nectarine as both are in flower early in the year when there are few pollinators about. Rosemary will lure the pollinators in and, having visited, they can feast on the nectarine flowers.

1. Start by adding a layer of fresh compost around your permanent plant. This will give both plants a nutrient boost.

2. Choose your plant for underplanting. Here I am using a mint.

3. Divide it into pieces that have some roots attached. Plant the pieces around the permanent planting and firm them in well.

4. Water the pieces in and return to harvest the underplanting regularly. Leave mint uncut – or only minimally cut – if you want it to flower and lure in the pollinators.

food on the move

Plants are not exactly nomadic things, but they only have a few needs, and as long as you can cater for those you can take them anywhere. The gardens in this chapter aren't just small, they are also mobile, and can be moved wherever they are most needed. On a small scale that can mean shifting a wheelbarrow garden to catch the sun, but on a larger scale it allows the gardener to take food production to the heart of the city, and near to the people who need the food.

the edible wheelbarrow

Fiona Blackmore is not used to having to garden in miniature. Pennard Plants, the nursery where she is a gardener, boasts 8,000 square metres (2 acres) of beautiful red-brick walled garden – more than enough space to play with plantings. But Fiona is aware that not many of their customers are in the same position. 'We take plants to lots of garden shows, and many of the customers have really small gardens and want to know which are the best plants for growing in a small space.' She found an old wheelbarrow in the grounds and decided it would be perfect for showing just how much can be done with a really tiny area. 'It's also easy to wheel on and off the truck and into place on our stand at the shows. It was perfect.'

She thinks a wheelbarrow planter could prove useful in less specific situations, too. 'There are lots of strong flavours in here that you might want to use when cooking outdoors, so you can wheel the barrow over to the barbecue. And in a small garden, you can easily wheel the barrow into the sun to stop these sun-loving plants from being in shade for some of the day.'

Fiona has chosen compact varieties, many of which are not widely available, so that they will grow happily in their small space for a number of years. 'I also looked for really aromatic, flavourful types. I wanted to show that the largest punch of flavour can be delivered by some of the smallest plants.'

Left: The edible wheelbarrow can be placed wherever Fiona most needs it.

Above: Tricolour sage, rosemary and thyme are among the highly flavoured crops in the barrow.

style and gardening notes

'It's not unusual to find an old wheelbarrow with holes in the bottom where the water has sat and the rust has kicked in,' says Fiona, 'but if yours has an intact base, then make a few holes with a drill for drainage, including at its very lowest point.'

Fiona had to drill the base of hers, and she then filled it with multi-purpose, peat-free compost and started planting. She has fitted an impressive number of plants into this tiny, mobile plot: Moroccan mint, golden oregano, thyme 'Faustini' (a particularly compact type), wild strawberries, oregano 'Compact Form', garlic chives, lemon verbena, lemon grass, rosemary, thyme 'Tabor' (a broad-leafed thyme), Tulbaghia 'Fairy Star' and chilli 'Gusto Purple'. 'As well as looking for compact types I was also looking for colourful leaves. Choosing the odd variegated variety makes a big difference to the look of a planter like this. It lights it up and stops the whole thing from looking dull green when nothing's in flower.'

Everything is planted directly into the compost except for the Moroccan mint, which is planted into a terracotta pot and then the whole pot is perched atop the compost. 'It needs its own pot because mint roots are very invasive. It would quickly swamp the other plants.'

Right: Tulbaghia is an onion relative with edible leaves and flowers.

Left: Mint is planted into its own pot and sunk into the compost.

Far right: Fiona planted up the wheelbarrow to show customers what can be done in a small space.

herby campervan companions

This is my campervan, and I like to take a tiny herb garden with me when I head off on jaunts. There isn't a great deal of complicated cooking goes on in there. If we are only off for a quick weekend trip, then it's just beans and eggs and a couple of rashers of bacon heated to crispy on the very handy cooker. But over the summer, as the camping hours start to clock up, I find that a family can't live on fry-ups alone and I settle into cooking something a little more complicated: the odd salad, a pasta sauce, a big, warming chilli con carne should the weather turn cool (and it always does). We're not talking great culinary feats here, but it's good to be able to make full use of my campervan's neat cooking facilities occasionally.

I love cooking with fresh herbs and after only a few trips away I started to miss them. It didn't take long for me to realise that it made perfect sense to create a little mobile 'garden' of herbs that could come along with us, nestled alongside the soy sauce, the chilli flakes and the other flavourful bottles and jars that I pack to help turn a bagful of farm-gate produce into a meal. I've chosen my favourite and most often-used herbs: oregano for pasta dishes, Greek basil for salads, and lemon verbena for instant, fresh, lemony herb teas or to sprinkle onto a fruit salad. They make all those al fresco meals taste even better.

Left: Delicious lemon verbena tea just takes a few leaves.

Right: Lia in her campervan.

style and gardening notes

Almost all herbs live very happily indeed in pots, so any would-be camping herb gardener should just plant those that they use most often. I felt it was important not to add too much extra weight to the already groaning campervan, so I transplanted my bought herbs from their terracotta pots into large catering-size tins and a few old tin kettles – fewer chances of breakages, too. All these herbs like plenty of drainage, so I punched holes in the bases of the containers and used a compost containing plenty of grit.

In transit the pots are wedged in among the other packing to stop them getting bashed about. As soon as we pull up somewhere for the weekend, they're released out into the fresh air, to settle in to their new temporary surroundings and to soak up whatever sunshine or showers the weekend has in store for us. As soon as we've got some water from the campsite tap, we give the herbs a dribble: you want to water them on arrival at the campsite, not just before you're setting off for home or you'll have water in your van.

Herbs love to be plucked: it stops them from growing leggy and encourages bushiness, so you really can make merry with your herbs and take as much of them as you like. Pick and add generously to everything you cook; it can only do the herbs good. Between trips, my campervan herb garden lives out in the back garden, recovering from its travels and growing new leaves.

Right: Taking herbs along for the ride opens up culinary possibilities.

Left: The mobile herb garden off on its latest trip.

out-of-the-truck thinking

Ian Cheney is a documentary maker who has made films about the state of the food industry in the USA, including the award-winning 'King Corn', for which he grew 4,000 square metres (1 acre) of corn in order to witness first hand the problems of growing this, America's most subsidised crop. 'Corn is the raw material for high-fructose corn syrup and countless processed foods, and it's been implicated in our epidemics of obesity and diabetes,' he says.

'After immersing myself in this world, I felt it was high time I tried planting a real garden of my own.' But having moved to New York City, Ian struggled to find land. 'I didn't own any land and all the community gardens were full, so I took a long, hard look at the 1986 Dodge my grandfather had given me when I graduated from college and decided to give truck farming a whirl.'

The truck farm worked brilliantly, with the first crops – lettuces and radishes – germinating within days. The truck quickly attracted attention from children in the neighbourhood, so Ian starting taking it around to local nursery schools. 'For many of the youngsters it was their first glimpse of food crops growing in soil. The reports back from the teachers were very enthusiastic.'

When Ian's long-time collaborator Curt Ellis moved to New York later that summer, the two friends set to work expanding the Truck Farm project into a fully-functioning, mobile education device, and started touring the truck – now planted up with tomatoes, calabrese and nasturtiums too – around schools far beyond the boundaries of NYC. They have since encouraged a community of truck gardeners across the USA to plant up their trucks and take them out to schools. Ian says: 'Truck farms have the power to engage people in out-of-the-box thinking about the way we grow food.'

Opposite: The fully planted-up truck garden.

Below: Sowing seeds directly into the back.

style and gardening notes

The design and installation of the truck farm was simple, and building it took less than a day once they had collected the materials – and all for less than $200. Donated green roof materials were used to line the base of the truck, to help excess water to drain away, and a lightweight soil was placed on top of this. Then they added a layer of normal compost on top for the seeds to be sown into, and placed a Perspex section across the back end of the truck so that children could see the growing plants.

Ian and Curt chose heritage seeds from Iowa's Seed Savers Exchange and sowed them direct. Once the seeds started to grow, Ian moved the truck farm to find shade on hot days, occasionally to borrow water from the hose spigot of the Italian restaurant down the block, and to dodge the street cleaners on Mondays and Fridays.

The truck farm has now been out on tour three seasons in a row, visiting schools all over the north-east. Despite a blown gasket in rural Connecticut, the old Dodge has fared well, and Ian and Curt have spoken to hundreds of school children and distributed thousands of seed packets. 'Each school visit was different and unique, but we were consistently impressed by the students' inquisitiveness, imagination and creativity. We are really out there to pass on a simple message: growing your own food is fun, easy, and rewarding, and you can do it anywhere.'

Opposite left: Climbing and taller plants are supported on strings strung between two canes.

Below left: Ian Cheney with his truck farm.

Left: A small greenhouse can be attached to the top to create warmer condition for the plants.

Below left: Basil grows well in the back of the truck.

Centre: Seeds germinate quickly.

Right: The truck can be moved around the neighbourhood to wherever the growing conditions are best.

self-contained food supply

Damien Chivialle, an artist and designer based in Zurich, has designed an entire farming system that can fit into a parking space. Damien became worried about the problems of feeding an ever-increasing urban population, and about the energy required to move food around cities, so he decided to do something about it.

He takes industrial containers and transforms them into tiny, self-regulating farms, designed to work in a city environment, and particularly in areas that would not traditionally be associated with growing food. The containers, or Urban Farm Units, are suited to growing over contaminated or otherwise unusable soil, or in a street environment. And perhaps more importantly, they take the growing food to where the consumers are, so cutting out polluting and costly transport.

Each Urban Farm Unit is self-watering, self-feeding and wholly organic. Essentially a greenhouse held in place on top of a container unit, it can produce fruits, vegetables and even fish within its tiny footprint. Since it was designed for an urban environment, it was important that the vulnerable part – the greenhouse – was up high and out of harm's reach. Additionally, the walls of the container are fairly solid and impenetrable once the unit is locked up. Crops are grown hydroponically in the greenhouse part of the unit, and freshwater fish are in large tanks down below, in the container part. 'The question for me is: can the consuming city become the producing city?' says Damien. 'That's why I designed these units. This is one way that it can.'

Left: The Urban Farm Unit is a self-sufficient food production unit, created for use in cities.

Opposite: It has been designed to fit into a standard parking space.

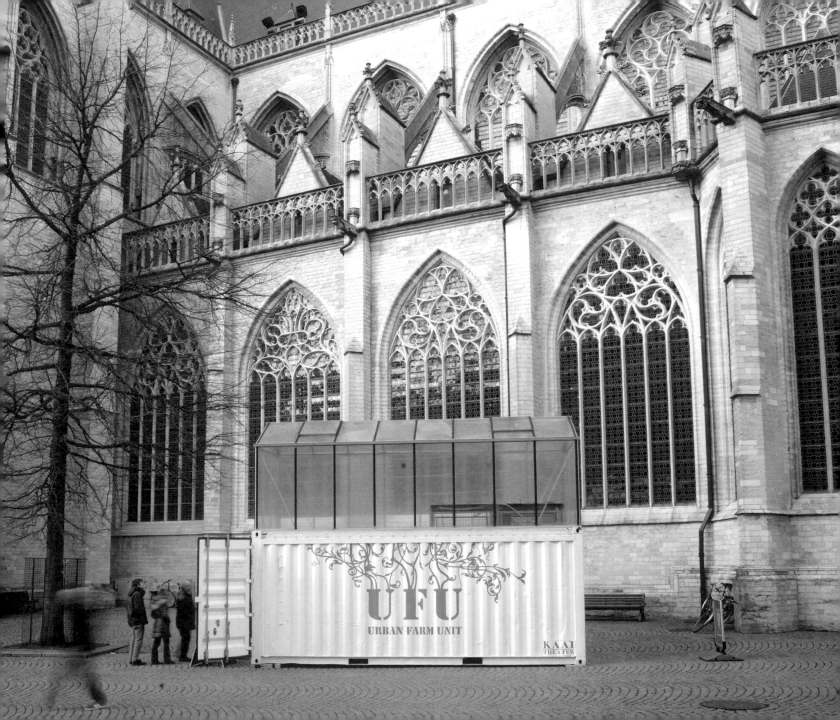

Top: The greenhouse is up high enough to be out of reach when the unit is locked up.

Above: When up and running the unit needs little outside input.

Right: Crops are grown in the greenhouse.

style and gardening notes

From the outside, the units look industrial and basic. Though there is lots of scope for decorating the outside, a container is always going to look like a container. It is inside where the complexities lie. In the base of the container are three large tanks containing freshwater fish. Water is fed from these tanks into a filter and purifier, where the fish excrement is broken down into minerals by bacteria. This water is then pumped up to the hydroponic pipes of the greenhouse.

No soil is used in this system; instead the roots of the plants in the greenhouse grow submerged in the nutrient-rich fish water. It is a closed water loop. No water is wasted: the water that is fed through the hydroponic pipes is then fed back to the fish tanks. No other fertiliser is needed either. 'And as long as the fish are given organic feed, all the products grown in the system will also be organic,' says Damien.

Already these units are growing food in unlikely spots in cities around the world. In Paris, one unit holds 160 plants and breeds carp. It produces enough food for ten people. The Rotterdam unit grows 320 plants, breeds perch and feeds 20 people, while three units in Istanbul hold 384 plants, breed tilapia, and produce enough food for 24 people. Brussels has gone for eels and Montreal for trout. It is not a bad result: fruit, vegetables and fish, all produced within a standard-sized parking space.

Left: The lower level contains large fish tanks.

get practical: feeding time

One of the tricky things about growing in pots is keeping fertility levels high. Many composts contain nutrients, but this is used up by the plant or leached away by watering within a few months. After that you need to keep regularly topping the plant up with nutrients. Here are a few ways to do it.

1. Comfrey is a useful plant for making fertiliser. It needs to be grown in the ground rather than in a pot, as its roots reach deep down into the soil searching for nutrients. You can create a strong, nutrient-rich comfrey tea by cutting some of the leaves, placing them in a lidded bucket and leaving them to rot down for a couple of months.

2. The liquid that is produced should be diluted, 1 part comfrey feed to 10 parts water, then watered in or sprayed on foliage as a foliar feed. It is high in potash so is particularly good for tomatoes and any other plants that you want to encourage to flower and fruit. Use it weekly during the growing season.

3. Over time, the compost in long-term plantings sinks and needs topping up. Adding a fresh layer will deliver a boost of nutrients, while also improving the soil so it holds on better to any nutrients that are applied.

4. Slow-release fertilisers such as chicken-manure pellets will keep your plant well fed over a spell of time so you don't have to keep using liquid fertiliser. Sprinkle them over the surface of the compost or soil at a rate of 50g (1¾oz) pellets to 1 square metre (8 square foot). Renew them every four to six weeks.

small talk

These are the tiniest of all of the gardens in this book, ranging from a hanging ball of lettuce up to a not-especially-gargantuan metre-square plot. Each of these mini gardens provides for a very specific purpose: one is purely there to provide cups of herbal tea for a garden office worker, one creates a supply of sprouts for snacking and stir fries and another keeps lettuce out of slugs' way and places it in the eyeline of intrigued children. If your only growing space is a windowsill, you can still grow something edible.

teatime at the shepherd's hut

'This is a place where I spend a lot of time,' says photographer and writer Mark Diacono of the shepherd's hut in his vegetable garden. 'It's where I write, and if I'm in the middle of a book, I might spend 60 hours a week here.'

Mark created his 'tea garden' as a treat to himself during these long writing sessions. 'I've got a little stove and a kettle in here and I can pick a few leaves from the steps, and make a really refreshing tea. It perks me up if I'm getting tired.'

Mark uses the herbs for more cerebral reasons, too. 'I love smells so I've chosen herbs that smell wonderful. I write about my garden and about the food I grow here. In fact, I bought the shepherd's hut so I could be in the middle of it all as I was writing. Having the scent of the herbs on my fingers as I write is another way of staying connected to the outside.'

Mark does not have much farther to go to cook up a writing-hut lunch. 'There's a Szechuan pepper plant at the bottom of the steps. I love the peppers and the crushed leaves are one of my favourite smells, so I would have it there even just to brush against it as I pass. But if I fancy, I can also take a few eggs from the chickens across the garden and make an omelette with plenty of crushed Szechuan pepper in it.'

Left: Mark on the steps of the shepherd's hut where he writes.

Above: Herbs that work well as herbal teas grow on the steps.

Right: The shepherd's hut is in Mark's vegetable garden.

Left: The herbs help Mark to feel immersed in the garden he is writing about.

Above: Szechuan pepper, for scent and omelettes.

style and gardening notes

Mark's favourite tea plant is lemon verbena. 'It makes a gorgeous tea with a very clean, fresh lemon taste but not at all harsh, and very sherbet-like. It's my "desert-island" herb. Everyone should have one.' He also sometimes combines it in the cup with Moroccan mint, one of several mints he keeps near at hand on the steps. 'Moroccan mint is the best mint for tea as it's so aromatic. A few leaves of lemon verbena and Moroccan mint work beautifully together.'

For a slightly different minty tea he goes for Tasmanian mountain mint. 'It's strongly aromatic, too, but it's a bit spicier than Moroccan mint.' He has a slightly different use for 'Kentucky Colonel' mint. 'This is the one for your mint juleps. Muddle the leaves in the bottom of the glass and add sugar syrup, bourbon and crushed ice. I try not to drink too many of these when I'm working.' Finally he grows basil mint, which makes a great addition to that Szechuan pepper omelette.

There's a pot of anise hyssop at the top of the steps, too: 'That's another great tea plant; its flavour is somewhere between aniseed and mint.' It also smells gorgeous and attracts bees and butterflies to this little corner of the garden.

The steps are in partial shade, so mint plants are the perfect choice. 'They like shade and they're best in pots, as they tend to spread if they're planted in the ground. As far as I'm concerned, they make for a very happy tea garden on my steps.'

Above left: Tasmanian mountain pepper has fabulously scented leaves.

Above centre: Mint 'Kentucky Colonel', for occasional mint juleps.

Above right: The steps are often in shade, and so suit Mark's mints perfectly.

archie and oscar's sprouting windowsill garden

It was only when he spotted his sons' unlikely fondness for alfalfa that Reuben Milne started growing sprouted seeds on a windowsill of their Bedfordshire home. 'The boys eat alfalfa by the fistful. It's strange but true. I knew how good sprouted seeds were for them so I thought I'd make the most of it by always having some on the go.' A just-sprouted seed is jam-packed with the sort of goodness that young boys are generally loath to ingest – amino acids, enzymes, vitamins, proteins and lots of fibre. So it is not surprising that Reuben decided to indulge his sons' unusual tastes.

'The other thing about sprouting seeds is that they're fun,' he says, 'and educational – though the boys don't realise that.' Sprouting seeds are very good for people with short attention spans. The windowsill sprout garden allows Archie, 6, and Oscar, 9, to enjoy the fruits of their gardening labours within a few days. 'They can start to see swelling and the beginning of germination almost immediately,' says Reuben. 'And within a day or two, the root tips start to emerge and they can eat them. Almost instant results!' Not all of the sprouts are scoffed raw; some are incorporated into the family's meals. 'I make a mean stir-fry,' says Reuben, 'so I particularly like growing my own bean sprouts. They don't come out like the ones from the supermarket – they're much smaller and nuttier – but they're a great addition all the same.'

Left: Chickpeas, brown lentils, alfalfa, mung beans and sunflower seeds sprout in Archie and Oscar's jars.

Right: The boys have covered them with colourful fabric, so that they look good on the windowsill.

style and gardening notes

To keep the boys' interest, Reuben encourages them to sprout their seeds in clear glass vases, jars and drinking glasses. That way they can see the entire process at work, from dormant seed to ready-to-eat sprout. All the containers sit proudly on the front windowsill. 'At the moment we're growing sunflower seeds, which produce big, green, mild, crunchy sprouts, and lentils. These are particularly tasty. And we always have some alfalfa on the go for when the boys get the munchies. I like using the sprouted mung beans in stir-fries, but the chickpeas are good, too. They're the chunkiest of the lot.'

Each batch of seeds is started off with an overnight soak. In the morning the boys put their tops on (they have made these out of scraps of colourful netting, held in place with elastic bands) and drain them. After this, the seeds need to be kept relatively dry, but washed every day. This 'waters' the sprouts and helps to keep them fresh. 'It's important to have an easy way of washing and draining them, particularly when kids are involved, otherwise it won't happen and the results aren't great,' says Reuben. 'This was the simplest method I found.' The seeds should not be left to sit in water or they will start to rot. 'The boys now know how to wash and drain them properly, and they take turns each day. The seeds have become almost like a pet that needs taking care of.'

Above: Oscar with his chickpea sprouts.

Below: The boys take it in turns to rinse and drain the sprouts daily.

Right: Archie loves alfalfa.

Far right: Sunflower seed sprouts are mild and crunchy.

a feast of hanging lettuces

The creative impulse that inspired Dawn Isaac's hanging lettuce ball came from an unfortunate juxtaposition of vegetable patch and box hedge. 'I made some new vegetable beds and as I've always loved the look of box hedges, I decided to edge the veg beds with them, not realising that snails would hide in the hedges and crawl out at night. The lettuces, in particular, didn't stand a chance.'

Raising lettuces high off the ground and out of reach of the slugs and snails is perhaps the only guaranteed way of protecting them from these voracious molluscs. Dawn has had perfect, untouched lettuce leaves ever since she constructed her little hanging garden.

The lettuce ball hangs in a corner of the garden that is well used by her children, and at a height where they, including Ava, aged 11, find it easy to care for the lettuces and harvest them. 'It's an odd thing and funny to look at. I wanted something that would intrigue them and make them smile,' says Dawn. She also hoped that by adding a slight element of comedy to her vegetable growing, she might entice her children to eat the foods that they are usually most averse to. 'They won't eat a salad. In fact, I can't get them to eat anything green indoors. But if they find it in the garden, it's a different story. They'll pick and eat it there and then, no problem. That's the way it is with the lettuce leaves, so I think it was worth the trouble.'

Left: Dawn and Ava caring for the lettuce ball.

style and gardening notes

The lettuce ball is created using two standard hanging baskets wired together. The baskets need lining with moss, so Dawn asked Ava to rake the moss out of the lawn, and they used that to carefully line both baskets. Two problems solved in one go. 'You could use hanging-basket liners just as easily,' she says, 'but if you've got your own source of moss and your own workforce, you may as well make use of them.' After lining, each hanging basket was balanced on top of an empty pot for filling. Dawn used compost mixed with a good scattering of water-retaining granules to prevent it from drying out too quickly.

She chose lettuce 'Green Salad Bowl' for its curved, sweet, mild, lime-coloured leaves, 'Lollo Biondo' for tightly curled green leaves, 'Lollo Rossa' for the same in dark purple, and 'Red Batavia' and 'Green Batavia', both of which have a slight nuttiness.

After filling the base of each basket with a little compost, Dawn and Ava pushed the roots of their plug plants through gaps made in the moss, and then secured them by adding more compost on top of the roots. 'The general idea is to get a roughly even spread of lettuces but it doesn't matter too much. As they fill out, they'll cover up any mistakes.'

Putting the two halves together is tricky and requires a couple of people and some fancy wiring, but it does not take long. Dawn finished by hanging her lettuce ball in partial shade, which prevents it from drying out too quickly and makes for softer, lusher leaves – all the better to tempt her children.

Left: Dawn chose a number of different coloured and textured leaves for the ball.

Left: The ball hangs low enough that Ava can water it herself.

Above: The leaves are untroubled by slugs and snails.

feisty veg that fend for themselves

In a sleepy village in Somerset, nursery owner Chris Smith has created a series of metre-square beds that show just how much can be grown in such a tiny area. One contains a tower of beans, and a second, herbs and leaves, but it is the third, the perennial bed, that is perhaps the most interesting. 'I'm away exhibiting at garden shows a lot during the summer. It means that things can get neglected, so I wanted these to be low-maintenance beds. The perennial bed has been the most successful. Most of the plants here will look after themselves until it's time to harvest at the end of the year,' he says.

To this end, Chris has chosen a brace of unusual perennial South-American tuber crops for this bed: ulluco has fleshy, low-growing leaves and produces colourful, potato-like tubers ('but without the diseases that potatoes get'); oca produces a spread of silvery-green clover-like leaves and tubers with a lemony flavour that can be eaten raw or cooked; yacon is the most architectural of the lot, with big, floppy, grey-green leaves, and large, sweet, fruity tubers with a crunchy texture, that can be eaten roasted or raw. In among these, Chris has planted a tripod of 'Crystal Lemon' cucumbers and a 'California Bell' pepper. It is a hugely productive little square. 'I wanted to show that any tiny patch of ground, any little bit of space – you can always make something of it and grow something delicious.'

Left: Chris next to his low-maintenance metre-square bed.

Above: A highly productive tripod of cucumber 'Crystal Lemon'.

Right: Ulluco produces potato-like tubers at the end of the season.

style and gardening notes

Chris has used the tripod of the cucumber supports to give this bed height and structure, but the yacon also lends a sculptural element that gives it a little more glamour than the average vegetable bed.

Although the tubers are perennials they are of the sort known as 'replant perennials'. They are frost-tender and so all are dug up at the end of the season. Some are then eaten but some are kept for replanting the following spring, after the frosts have passed – hence the name 'replant perennials'.

The plants grow healthy leaves all season long but only start to form tubers as the days shorten, so you need to leave them in the ground as long as possible. In fact, since the tubers swell in the couple of weeks following the collapse of the foliage, you can even leave them to get a light frosting, then gather them afterwards. Chris stores the tubers for replanting in paper bags in a cool, dry, frost-free porch.

The trick to growing these plants in such a small area, says Chris, is plenty of feeding and good compost. This bed is in its first year, so the compost contains plenty of nutrients, but Chris has still fed with seaweed fertiliser as the year has gone on. Next year he will top the bed up with nutrient-rich, fresh compost and will continue feeding. 'That's really the key to getting good crops out of a tiny area,' he says, as he looks forward to a bumper crop of tubers after a summer of neglect. 'In fact,' he adds, 'this would make a brilliant planting for a school garden. The kids can harvest their crops when they're back at school in autumn. That should make them look forward to coming back!'

Left: The tubers of oca can be eaten cooked or raw and have a slight lemon taste.

get practical: oriental greens from a butler's sink

Vegetable gardens often grind to a halt come winter, but they need not. There are a number of great crops you can grow through the cold months, and among the best are the Oriental leafy greens. They come in a range of different textures, colours and flavours, from mild, white-stemmed pak choi through to deepest red, peppery mustard 'Red Frills'. Planted in late summer or early autumn, these Oriental greens will bulk up into chunky rosettes that can be harvested for salads while small, and for stir-fries when larger. A butler's sink is a good canvas on which to arrange them into a colourful, leafy, winter tapestry. I recommend 25 plants for a sink measuring 60cm x 45cm (24in x 18in).

1. Place a piece of broken terracotta pot over the plughole of the sink to stop it from clogging, then fill the sink with good, peat-free, multipurpose compost. Firm the compost down. It should sit a few centimetres/inches below the edge of the sink to leave room for watering.

2. You will need small plug plants of some different varieties of Oriental greens, either grown from seed sown a few weeks before, or bought. I arranged mine in a pattern, starting with a row diagonally across the middle of the sink.

3. Next, I filled in with more plants either side of the diagonal. A completely random pattern could look just as good, but whatever you do, leave plenty of space for growth and for the plants to fill out.

4. When all the plug plants are in place, firm them in and water well. Water occasionally and harvest when the leaves are 15cm (6in) or longer.

get practical: make a winter herb terrarium

Terrariums were a huge fad in the 1970s, when gardeners would fill them with humidity-loving ferns and place them on their smoked-glass tables in their Harvest Gold-painted sitting rooms. But terrariums slipped out of fashion along with macramé pot holders, which means they are reasonably easy to track down. They are also very pretty things and surprisingly useful for giving a little outdoor protection to winter plantings. I have mine outside the back door and use it for planting out hardy winter annual herbs, such as chervil, parsley and coriander. These all grow perfectly well outdoors, but produce softer, more tempting foliage with the added protection of the terrarium's little glass facets.

1. Few terrariums have drainage holes, so start by placing a layer of horticultural grit over the base, then a layer of 'activated charcoal' (used in water filters, it helps to stop the compost from getting smelly, which is essential where there are no drainage holes), then a few centimetres of compost.

2. You will need little herb plants a few centimetres tall and ready to plant out, either sown a few weeks earlier or bought in. Plant them firmly into the compost.

3. Water in carefully. You want all the compost to be moist but do not want the plants sitting in a pool of water. Throughout the winter, use your fingertips to check how dry the compost is every week or so, and sprinkle on a little water only when it is needed.

4. Snip fresh leaves all winter long, always leaving the growing point at the base of the plant intact, so it can grow again.

a capital investment

Tiny-scale gardens aren't just reserved for the amateur gardener. Businesses are getting in on the act too, realising that small in stature can also mean huge in taste. Everybody wants flavour, and micro greens provide tiny explosions of it which detonate in your mouth, even though they are mere centimetres tall. Mushroom farms can be grown in a corner of a kitchen to provide a succession of harvest-fresh mushrooms. Follow the examples of these businesses and make the most of the big flavours that come from the tiniest of plots.

micros at le manoir

Raymond Blanc's kitchen garden at his two Michelin star restaurant, Belmond Le Manoir aux Quat'Saisons in Oxfordshire, is not tiny. It extends over 8,000 square metres (2 acres) and produces 90 types of vegetables and 70 varieties of herbs, all of which are put to work daily in the kitchen. However, there is a tiny corner of one polytunnel that punches well above its weight when it comes to flavour, and that is the table where the micro leaves grow.

'Micros are just tiny seedlings of edible plants,' says head gardener Anne-Marie Owens, 'but by harvesting when the plants are so small – rather than letting them grow to maturity – you get a really concentrated, strong, clean taste. The chefs absolutely love them. They use them as a garnish on a great many of the dishes.'

In fact they are so keen on their micros, that Anne-Marie harvests between eight and 12 trays a day, delivering them to the kitchen door at 11.45am just before service. 'The micro herbs are designed into the dishes from the very start,' says Anne-Marie. 'The chefs tell us the sort of flavour they're looking for – hot, spicy, fresh, savoury – and we'll give them a list of the micros we can offer, given the time of year. They select from this and then we grow them for them.'

'It's a major operation here, because the kitchens serve 1,000 meals a week, but it doesn't have to be. If you've got a bit of seed left over at the end of the season, and a spot on a windowsill, you can get exactly the same huge flavours that we produce.'

Left: Micros of beetroot, coriander, purple basil, red mustard and pea.

Right: Le Manoir dedicates plenty of space in one of its large polytunnels to its micros.

Far right: Coriander micros have a strong, clear flavour.

style and gardening notes

'We sow seed thickly across the seed trays, water them and then cover them to keep them dark,' says Anne-Marie. The cover emulates covering them with compost but 'if they're covered with compost, the seedlings can lift the compost up as they grow, rather than grow through it. We don't want to send compost into the kitchen.' As soon as the seeds germinate, the covers are removed, and the seedlings are grown on for 10 to 14 days, depending on the plant and the season.

Many of the plants grown as micros are herbs, and Anne-Marie ranks dill, coriander and anise hyssop among her favourites. But other crops are also grown: watercress micros are strongly peppery, beetroots have an earthy flavour and a good colour on the plate, and radish has a hot kick. 'Celery is the micro that perhaps illustrates best of all how good micros can be. It's got a strong celery taste but it's also clear and clean. I love it.'

When it comes to harvesting, Anne-Marie recommends cutting just before you eat. 'They start to turn brown within the hour. When the weather's hot, I might harvest them right outside the kitchen door. Use a sharp pair of scissors and try to harvest them into something wide and shallow such as an old ice-cream carton, so they're not piled up on top of each other too much. They're easily crushed. The chefs lay them on damp tissue paper in trays in the fridge until they're needed, to keep them as fresh as possible.' The micro leaves may only be tiny, but in this garden and kitchen, they're revered.

Far left: Fennel seedlings almost ready for harvest.

Centre: Pea shoots have a fresh, strongly pea-like taste.

Left: Celery is one of Anne-Marie's favourite plants to use as a micro.

fungi from the far west

The Garrone family business, Far West Fungi, may produce thousands of mushrooms a week on their 60,000 square foot mushroom farm in Monterey County, California, but they still think that mushroom growing is perfect for tiny-scale growing. 'Our mini kits use exactly the same process as we do in our farm,' says Ian Garrone, who runs the family's shop in San Francisco. 'The first flush of mushrooms is guaranteed, and if you treat the mini farm right you can get up to a pound of mushrooms from each.'

The kits take the form of a brick of sawdust and rice bran, high pressure steam-treated and then inoculated with either shiitake mushroom or tree oyster mushroom mycelium. They are then grown on in one of the farm's grow rooms and put out for sale when they are a week or so from producing their first flush of mushrooms.

Far West Fungi started life growing and selling only button mushrooms, but its 21 years have seen it change direction to cater for the 'niche organic market' of San Francisco. 'We realised that all of these fresh mushrooms were being imported from China so we branched out with shiitakes, then a few other different types. The business has changed completely. Now we don't even grow button mushrooms,' says owner John Garrone. They do however grow ten types of mushrooms themselves and sell at least 70 different kinds. 'Even if you think you don't like mushrooms we will find something for you. There is a mushroom for everyone,' says Ian.

Left: The mini farms grow well in beautiful glass bell jars.

Right: Ian Garrone in the shop.

Opposite: The shop sells many of the mushrooms grown at the farm.

style and gardening notes

Shiitake are the easiest to try at home, says Ian, and if you don't have access to one of his kits it is often fairly easy to track down shiitake plugs, which you can use to inoculate logs yourself: 'They are the most durable and the best to start off with, particularly if you have less than perfect indoor growing conditions. They are also the longest lasting of our mini farms, and will produce three to four crops over a five-month period. But really you want to grow them because they have a unique flavour, perhaps the finest of any mushroom.' His second recommendation for beginners is tree oyster mushrooms, which are succulent and shellfish-like.

The kits are kept in plastic bags with punched air holes to keep the air around the developing mushrooms humid. 'And in the shop we place the kits under glass bell jars, partly because it looks beautiful,' says Ian, but if you try this at home the bell jars need to be lifted on small blocks of wood so that there is some air movement around the kits. Ideal conditions are cool rooms away from draughts or direct sunlight. A spray bottle misting the inside of the bag or bell jar is all the watering they need, and once the mushrooms have started to grow they should be ready to pick within a few days. Ian is convinced they are a great crop for those with little space. 'They take up very little room and are easy to grow, and produce a delicious, unusual, abundant crop.'

Below: An impressive display in the San Francisco shop.

Opposite, above: Porcini have a rich nutty flavour and firm, buttery texture.

Opposite, middle: A mixed tray of mushrooms.

Opposite, below: Fresh mushrooms are harvested daily.

Opposite, right: The coral-like pink oyster mushroom.

GO GIANTS!
GIANT PORCINI
14— lb.

get practical: cut-and-come-again leaves

The baby leaves that you buy in bags from the supermarket are really easy to grow yourself. They are particularly well suited to those with small gardens (or no garden) because – as the name 'cut-and-come-again' suggests – you will get several flushes of crop-worthy leaves from the same plant. You cut them once they have grown to a few centimetres/inches high, but you must always leave the growing tip at the base intact so it can grow again. Suitable plants include lettuces, rocket, chard, beetroot, Oriental greens and all of the annual herbs.

1. Choose a wide, shallow container such as a seed tray or an old colander, and fill it with multipurpose compost. Sprinkle the seeds across the surface according to the packet directions.

2. Sprinkle a little more compost over the seeds and then water in.

3. When the seedlings reach a few centimetres/inches in height, cut them, taking care to not cut too low.

4. These are one of the few crops that are best not eaten immediately as they benefit from a spell of 'conditioning' in water. Plunge the leaves into a bowl of cold water and leave them for half an hour, then drain them and shake them dry. Place them in a plastic bag in the fridge until required.

watering holes

Build a floating orchard on a boat, or create a whole eco system within an old, cracked swimming pool: nowhere is out of bounds. The unlikely-seeming, small edible gardens in this chapter have all been created on or around water, all making use of spaces that had previously seemed out of the reach of any gardener. It takes a certain amount of ingenuity and a lot of determination to turn such spots into productive vegetable and fruit gardens, but the returns are great.

on vous raconte des salades

let's talk about lettuce

The display of angled, tent-like structures, earth and lettuce at the floating *hortillonages* gardens in Amiens, northern France, is part political statement, part architectural gymnastics, part greenhouse. The installation was commissioned for the city's annual *Art, Villes et Paysage* (Art, Towns and Countryside) festival, and was built by architects Atelier Altern. 'We decided to use two small, abandoned islands to tell people about old, forgotten salad varieties,' says Sylvain Morin, one of the architects working on the project. The *hortillonages* are a series of small vegetable gardens linked by canals and covering an area of roughly 300 acres. They are thought to have been gardened since the Middle Ages.

The spot where Atelier Altern chose to build their installation has, appropriately enough, a name that translates as 'Salad Harbour'. On the bank – visitors can view this strange and beautiful lettuce house from the boats that carry them around the ancient gardens – the architects placed a plaque reading 'On vous raconte des salades', which roughly translates as 'Let's talk about lettuce'.

Their creation is a beautiful twisted structure filled with a number of heirloom, open-pollinated varieties of lettuce. Many of these are no longer widely grown in France, thanks to modern agriculture's rejection of older, more variable varieties and its preference for newer, far more standardised F1 hybrids. The architects have made the most of their skills and of this opportunity to draw attention in a most striking way to an interesting aspect of vanishing agricultural diversity.

Above: The bank upon which the installation was created was previously known as the 'Salad Harbour'.

Right: The structure is sculptural but also functional, as it shades the lettuces from the heat of the sun.

style and gardening notes

Eleven slightly varying pentagon-shaped frames were built from timber, then netting was stretched taut over some of the frames and the frames were set on the bare earth. Once weeded and composted, the earth was planted up with lettuces, spaced fairly closely so as to create a green carpet of lettuces once the plants were mature.

The *hortillonages* may be known as 'floating gardens' but they are in fact built up from mud and silt that has been excavated from the canals over hundreds of years. All manure and compost has to be brought in by small boat, so it is hard to improve the soil and make it more water-retentive. These factors combine to make the soil occasionally very dry, so Atelier Altern's installation needs regular watering despite being surrounded by water.

It is the slight differences between the shapes of the pentagons that give the structure its twisted appearance. While the white net covering adds greatly to the installation's looks, it also happens to be perfect for the plants. Lettuces don't like full sun. They bolt in the heat, running quickly to flower and then to seed, rather than producing lots of juicy, mild leaves. The leaves that are produced during bolting can be bitter. Since the net covering is only partial, it allows lots of air movement, which helps to keep the temperature down, yet also provides plenty of shade. Unlikely as it may seem, this beautiful sculpture is actually the perfect place for growing lettuce.

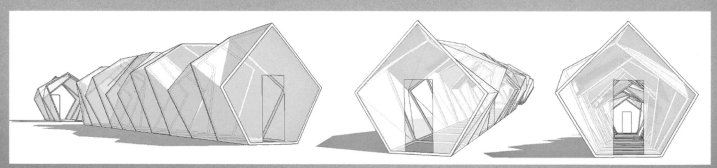

Above: The lettuces were planted out as small plants.

Left: Designs for the structure.

Opposite, above: Gaps in the fabric allow for good airflow.

Opposite, left: Heritage varieties were sown to demonstrate the declining diversity of lettuces in France.

floating orchard by tower bridge

Off the south bank of the River Thames, close to Tower Bridge, bobs a very unusual garden square. 'The idea came from a boat – a Thames lighter that we'd got moored here,' says moorings owner Nick Lacey. 'There was silt in the bottom and all sorts of things had seeded in it. It was like a floating garden. It was so intriguing that I decided to see what I could do with the idea.'

Now, three huge collar barges, joined together in a C-shape, form the basis for his floating garden square, with other 'garden barges' leading to it from the bank. There are seven of them altogether. They are the permanent moorings, and other craft moor up to them. 'I wanted each of the barges to have its own character,' says Nick, so one is filled with soft perennials and grasses, another, with its large box hedge, has an air of formality, while yet another is a sea of yellow rudbeckias.

Perhaps the most intriguing though, if only for its improbability, is the orchard barge, filled with large, healthy medlar trees that you would be proud to have grown on land. Apple trees, crab apples and quinces also grow here, and in among them are strawberries, tomatoes, herbs, and even a couple of beehives. 'The tidal range here is 7m (23ft),' says Nick, 'and we're continually moving, particularly when the ferries go past. It can become quite rough but it doesn't seem to bother the bees at all that their home moves up and down so dramatically.' Brimming with health and laden with fruit, the medlars seem equally at ease with their unusual situation.

Left: Nick with one of his floating apple trees.

Right: Pots of herbs are clustered together around the barges.

Opposite, top left: The gardens are an oasis within central London.

Opposite, top right: Just one spit of soil supports impressively lush growth.

Opposite, bottom left: Flowers mingle with the fruit trees.

Opposite, bottom right: Despite its central location, the community is strongly affected by the tides, and the garden experiences the high light levels and lack of frost often seen in coastal areas.

style and gardening notes

'There is only about one spit (a spade's depth) of soil here, so it's amazing that the medlar trees have grown as well as they have,' says Nick. 'Bringing the soil in for the gardens was an epic operation. Thirty-five tonnes came in by barge.' That was the obvious way to go about such a delivery for a community that is turned more towards the water than the land. Domestic rubbish is collected by barge and when a baby was born on one of the houseboats, the midwife arrived on a Royal National Lifeboat Institution (RNLI) boat.

The big, open-bottomed barges were boarded over to create the bases of the gardens, leaving living space beneath. Each then had its soil delivered and was planted up. The success of the plantings on such a small amount of soil seems to be mainly down to a drip irrigation watering system. 'For London, we get a lot of sun, but also a lot of wind,' says Nick, so plants have the potential to dry out quickly. But the proximity of such a large body of water has a mitigating effect on the temperature in the gardens, a fact borne out by a sprig of the tender *Geranium madarense*, which has seeded itself on one of the barges where it now grows quite happily. 'With the strength of the tides and the mildness of the temperatures, it feels estuarial here. We may be in the centre of London, but we're very much governed by the sea.'

Right: Compost bins and beehives nestle in the floating gardens.

swimming pool food factory

The day after Dennis and Danielle McClung completed the purchase of their new house, Dennis set about turning the old, cracked swimming pool into a greenhouse. 'I'd made a plan to change my life and live as self-sufficiently as possible, and I wanted to make the pool a part of that. I'd made a paper model of what I wanted to do with it, so that first day I just built a frame and covered it with UV plastic.' He filled the new sunken greenhouse with buckets planted up with crops, but in the heat of the Arizona summer, soon found he had to water five or six times a day.

After much experimenting he found that the key was to turn to a combination of hydroponics (growing plants entirely in fertilised water) and aquaponics (growing fish for food). In this 5m x 10m (16ft x 30ft) space, Dennis has created a 'closed loop' system that requires very little in the way of input, and yet provides a large proportion of his family's food. The five-year plan is working: 'Thanks to the garden pool we are self-sufficient above and beyond anything we could ever have imagined within city limits.'

The garden pool soon attracted attention: 'I started showing my friends and family, and next thing I know, all of their friends were asking and friends of friends, too. So many folks were interested that I started a meet-up group and organised tours – and I'm still doing that five years later. The garden pool has been a wonderful journey for me and my family.'

Left: Chillies growing in the garden pool.

Right: Dennis and Danielle grow a wide range of edible plants in their garden pool.

style and gardening notes

Central to the success of the system is the pond, created by filling the 'deep end' of the pool with water. Here Dennis breeds tilapia fish, which the family eat. He also has a raised area sited directly above the pond, where his chickens roost at night. Their droppings fall into the pond and make it high in nutrients, and this rich water is fed around the pipes to water and feed the plants. 'We reuse 90 per cent of our water. In the desert climate where we live, that's really important.' A solar-powered pump automatically draws the water up through the system to water the fruits and vegetables, then gravity takes the water back to the tilapia pond.

'The garden pool is a controlled environment that helps us grow an abundance of food all year round, even in our desert conditions. I'm not fighting the climate, or the weeds, birds or bugs. It makes gardening so much easier.'

He grows asparagus, mint, bok choi, oregano, parsley, cabbage and many other vegetables. The easiest plants are basil, lettuce, tomatoes and swiss chard. 'The only things that don't thrive in here are drought-tolerant desert plants,' but he can grow those outside.

'The garden pool needs very little input from us. We let the chickens in and out of the roosting area daily. We also check on the water flow to all the grow areas and we make sure there are no blockages. We get new seeds started and tend to the seedlings. With just this little amount of work we get an extraordinary amount of produce. It's amazing.'

Left: Cool-loving plants such as salad leaves will grow well here.

Above: The guttering that carries water from the pool to all of the plants.

Left: Fish-fertilised water is pumped through the system to water and feed all of the plants.

get practical: water rules

Keeping your plants well watered is perhaps the single thing that will make the difference between a successful container garden and a failing one. Plants in pots need lots of water. They have very limited access to rain and only to that which falls directly on them, most of which bounces off the leaves. So even during rainy times it is important to have a system for keeping them watered. And it must be a simple system or, especially if you have lots of pots, you are unlikely to keep it up long term.

1. A drip irrigation system is a bit fiddly to install but once it is in place, every plant pot connected to it will be watered with the turn of a tap. A series of thin hoses is connected to a central hose and from there to a tap. The thin hoses run across the surface of your pots and you add a drip attachment to the end of each. With the tap turned on, water slowly drips out into the pot.

2. To save you lugging water from indoors, set up a water butt to collect water from a downpipe. They come in all shapes and sizes – some tall and slim, some in brightly coloured plastic, and some, like mine, that look like a big terracotta pot – and they are far easier and cheaper to install than a garden tap.

3. Tomatoes are very thirsty plants so it pays to make them easy to water right from the start. Cut the bottom off a plastic water bottle and 'plant' it upside down alongside the tomato plant. Water straight into the bottle. The narrow bottle-neck will help to channel the water where it is needed. If you use a bottle with a sports cap left open, the water will slow to a gentle trickle, which will be even more beneficial.

4. If your pots have dried out, it is tempting to just slosh loads of water on them. But it is better for the plants if they are watered gradually. Ice cubes are perfect: as the ice slowly melts, the water seeps into the compost. They are particularly useful for popping into the surface of dried-out hanging baskets.

useful addresses

The tiny veg gardeners' businesses and blogs

Nell Nile
artist in chalks, pastels and ceramics www.nellnile.co.uk

The Shed Builder
Joel Bird builds bespoke sheds, outhouses, garden rooms and studios www.joelbird.com/theshedbuilder

Roof Top Veg Plot
Wendy Shillam blogs about gardening on her Fitzrovia rooftop at www.rooftopvegplot.com

Golightly Gardens
Penny Golightly blogs about gardening on a budget and in a small space at www.golightlygardens.com

Plant Lock Planters
Planters that double as bicycle locks, from www.frontyardcompany.co.uk/products/plantlock.html King Henry's Walk

Community Garden
award-winning community garden in Islington. For information on open days and events see www.khwgarden.org.uk

My Tiny Veg Plot
Gillian Carson's blog about gardening in Portland, Oregon mytinyplot.com

Tiny Trowels
a gardening group for pre-schoolers at Windmill Hill City Farm, Bristol www.windmillhillcityfarm.org.uk under the umbrella of Incredible Edible Bristol ediblebristol.org.uk

Anni's Perennial Veggies
blog written by Anni Kelsey on her experiments with small-scale perennials vegetable growing annisveggies.wordpress.com

Abundance London
the organisation behind the Chiswick Library, also concerned with picking and distributing unwanted and unpicked fruit http://www.abundancelondon.com/

Send a Cow
organisation dedicated to spreading small-scale farming techniques such as keyhole gardening through communities in Africa. There is lots of information about creating a keyhole garden of your own on the website www.sendacow.org.uk

Pennard Plants
Somerset nursery specialising in unusual edibles www.pennardplants.com

Truck Farm
New York-based food and film project that includes school outreach programmes. The website at www.truckfarm.org contains lots of information on creating your own truck farm.

Urban Farm Units
blog and website of UFU designer Damien Chivialle 20footurbanfarm.blogspot.com

Otter Farm
blog and website of Mark Diacono, garden and food writer and this book's photographer. His Otter Farm Shop sells seed and plants www.otterfarm.co.uk

Little Green Fingers
Dawn Isaac blogs about gardening with children at www.littlegreenfingers.typepad.com

Belmond Le Manoir aux Quatre Saisons
home of amazing vegetable gardens dedicated to producing flavourful produce for its two Michelin Star restaurant. The gardens are open to guests www.belmond.com/le-manoir-aux-quat-saisons-oxfordshire/

Far West Fungi
US source of mini mushroom farms and fresh and dried mushrooms www.farwestfungi.com

Atelier Altern
French landscape architects www.atelieraltern.com

Tower Bridge Moorings
floating garden square. See website for open days www.towerbridgemoorings.co.uk

Garden Pool
non-profit organisation and community concerned with turning old garden swimming pools into growing spaces gardenpool.org

Acknowledgments

I would like to thank all at Pavilion who have seen this book through from concept to completion, Fiona Holman and Nicola Newman in particular. Thanks to Hilary Mandleberg for her sharp editing eye, and to Laura Russell and Bet Ayer for the book's beautiful and clear design.

Mark Diacono's pictures are a joy as ever, and I would also like to thank him for his masterful timetabling and scheduling skills and for hours of driving, without which it would have been impossible for us to visit so many of the gardens in this book. My greatest thanks must go to the gardeners themselves who all gave so generously of their time and their thoughts on growing in small spaces. I would also like to thank the many gardeners who put themselves and their gardens forward who could not be included due to space restrictions or logistics. I am hugely grateful for your offers, as I am to those people who took the time to pass on contacts and ideas for possible gardeners to include in this book. Twitter and facebook users can be quite fantastically helpful.

Finally love and thanks to Michael, Rowan and Meg, for sparing me for the visiting of these gardens and the writing of this book through the precious summer holidays.